# HOW I LEARNED TO
# LET MY WORKERS
# LEAD

Harvard Business Review

*CLASSICS*

# HOW I LEARNED TO LET MY WORKERS LEAD

## Ralph Stayer

Harvard Business Press
Boston, Massachusetts

Published in the *Harvard Business Review* in 1990

Reprint #8318

Library of Congress Cataloging-in-Publication Data
Stayer, Ralph C.
    How I learned to let my workers lead / Ralph Stayer.
        p. cm.–(Harvard business review classics)
    ISBN 978-1-4221-3845-8 (pbk. : alk. paper)
1.  Leadership. 2.  Management–Employee participation.
3.  Employee motivation. I.  Title.
    HD57.7.S7249 2009
    658.4′092–dc22

                                                    2009010479

The paper used in this publication meets the requirements of the
American National Standard for Permanence of Paper for Publica-
tions and Documents in Libraries and Archives Z39.48-1992.

## THE HARVARD BUSINESS REVIEW CLASSICS SERIES

Since 1922, *Harvard Business Review* has been a leading source of breakthrough ideas in management practice—many of which still speak to and influence us today. The HBR Classics series now offers you the opportunity to make these seminal pieces a part of your permanent management library. Each volume contains a groundbreaking idea that has shaped best practices and inspired countless managers around the world—and will change how you think about the business world today.

# HOW I LEARNED TO
# LET MY WORKERS
# LEAD

In 1980, I was the head of a successful family business—Johnsonville Sausage—that was in great shape and required radical change.

Our profits were above the average for our industry, and our financial statements showed every sign of health. We were growing at a rate of about 20% annually, with sales that were strong in our home state of Wisconsin and steadily rising in Minnesota, Michigan, and Indiana. Our quality was high.

We were respected in the community.
I was making a lot of money.

And I had a knot in my stomach that wouldn't go away. For one thing, I was worried about competition. We were a small, regional producer with national competitors who could outpromote, outadvertise, and underprice us any time they chose.

In addition to our big national competitors, we had a host of local and regional producers small enough to provide superior service to customers who were virtually their neighbors. We were too big to have the small-town advantage and too small to have advantages of national scale. Our business was more vulnerable than it looked.

What worried me more than the competition, however, was the gap between potential and performance. Our people didn't seem to care. Every day I came to work and saw people so bored by their jobs that they made thoughtless, dumb mistakes. They mislabeled products or added the wrong seasonings or failed to mix them into the sausage properly. Someone drove the prongs of a forklift right through a newly built wall. Someone else ruined a big batch of fresh sausage by spraying it with water while cleaning the work area. These were accidents. No one was deliberately wasting money, time, and materials; it was just that people took no responsibility for their work. They showed up in the morning, did halfheartedly what they were told to do, and then went home.

Now, I didn't expect them to be as deeply committed to the company as I was. I owned it, and they didn't. But how could we survive a serious competitive challenge with this low level of attentiveness and involvement?

## GETTING TO POINTS B AND A

In 1980, I began looking for a recipe for change. I started by searching for a book that would tell me how to get people to care about their jobs and their company. Not surprisingly, the search was fruitless. No one could tell me how to wake up my own work force; I would have to figure it out for myself.

And yet, I told myself, why not? I had made the company, so I could fix it. This was an insight filled with pitfalls but it *was* an insight: the fault was not someone else's, the fault was mine.

Of course, I hadn't really built the company all alone, but I had created the management style that kept people from assuming responsibility. Of course, it was counterproductive for me to own all the company's problems by myself, but in 1980 every problem did, in fact, rest squarely on my shoulders, weighing me down and—though I didn't appreciate it at the time—crippling my subordinates and strangling the company. If I was going to fix what I had made, I would have to start by fixing myself. In many ways that was my good luck, or, to put the same thought another way, thank God I was the problem so I could be the solution.

As I thought about what I should do, I first asked myself what I needed to do to achieve the company's goals. But what *were* the company's goals? What did I really want Johnsonville to be? I didn't know.

This realization led me to a second insight: nothing matters more than a goal. The most important question any manager can ask is, "In the best of all possible worlds, what would I really want to happen?"

I tried to picture what Johnsonville would have to be to sell the most expensive sausage in the industry and still have the biggest market share. What I saw in my mind's eye was definitely not an organization where I made all the decisions and owned all the problems. What I saw was an organization where people took responsibility for their own work, for the product, for the company as a whole. If that happened, our product and service quality would improve, our margins would rise, and we could reduce costs and successfully enter new markets. Johnsonville would be much less vulnerable to competition.

The image that best captured the organizational end state I had in mind for Johnsonville was a flock of geese on the wing. I didn't want an organizational chart with traditional lines and boxes, but a "V" of individuals who knew the common goal, took turns leading, and adjusted their structure to the task at hand. Geese fly in a wedge, for instance, but land in waves. Most important, each individual bird is responsible for its own performance.

With that end state in mind as Point B, the goal, I turned to the question of our starting point, Point A. Johnsonville was financially successful, but I was dissatisfied with employee attitudes. So I conducted an attitude survey to find out what people thought about their jobs and the company and to get an idea of how they perceived the company's attitude toward them. I knew there was less commitment than I wanted, but I was startled all the same to find that Johnsonville attitudes were only average—no better than employee attitudes at big, impersonal companies like General Motors.

At first I didn't want to believe the survey, and I looked for all kinds of excuses. The methodology was faulty. The questions were poorly worded. I didn't want to admit that we had an employee motivation problem because I didn't know how to deal with that. But however strong the temptation, the mistakes and poor performance were too glaring to ignore.

The survey told me that people saw nothing for themselves at Johnsonville. It was a job, a means to some end that lay outside the company. I wanted them to commit themselves to a company goal, but they saw little to commit to. And at that stage, I still couldn't see that the biggest obstacle to changing their point of view was me. Everything I had learned and experienced to that point had convinced me that anything I didn't do myself would not be done right. As I saw it, my job was to create the agenda and then motivate "them" to carry it out.

In fact, I expected my people to follow me the way buffalo follow their leader—blindly. Unfortunately, that kind of leadership model almost led to the buffalo's extinction. Buffalo hunters used to slaughter the herd by finding and killing the leader. Once the leader was dead, the rest of the herd stood around waiting for instructions that never came, and the hunters could (and did) exterminate them one by one.

I realized that I had been focused entirely on the financial side of the business—margins, market share, return on assets—and had seen people as dutiful tools to make the business grow. The business had grown—nicely—and that very success was my biggest obstacle to change. I had made all the decisions about purchasing, scheduling, quality, pricing, marketing, sales, hiring, and all the rest of it. Now the very things that had brought me success—my centralized control, my aggressive behavior, my authoritarian business practices—were creating the environment that made me so unhappy. I had been Johnsonville Sausage, assisted by some hired hands who, to my annoyance, lacked commitment. But why should they make a commitment to Johnsonville? They had no stake in the company and no power to make decisions or control their own work. If I wanted to improve results, I had to increase their involvement in the business.

This was an insight that I immediately misused. Acting on instinct, I ordered a change. "From now on," I announced to my management team, "you're all responsible for making your own decisions." I went from authoritarian control to authoritarian abdication. No one had asked for more responsibility; I forced it down their throats. They were good soldiers, and they did their best, but I had trained them to expect me to solve their problems. I had nurtured their inability by expecting them to be incapable; now they met my expectations with an inability to make decisions unless they knew which decisions I wanted them to make.

After more than two years of working with them, I finally had to replace all three top managers. Worst of all, I now see that in a way they were right. I didn't really *want* them to make independent decisions. I wanted them to make the decisions I would have made. Deep down, I was still in love with my own control; I was just making people guess what I wanted instead of telling them. And yet I had to replace those three managers. I needed people who didn't guess so well, people who couldn't read my mind, people strong enough to call my bluff and seize ownership of Johnsonville's problems whether I "really" wanted to give it up or not.

I spent those two years pursuing another mirage as well—detailed strategic and tactical

plans that would realize my goal of Johnsonville as the world's greatest sausage
maker. We tried to plan organizational structure two to three years before it would be
needed—who would be responsible for what
and who would report to whom, all carefully
diagramed in boxes and lines on charts.
Later I realized that these structural changes
had to grow from day-to-day working reali-
ties; no one could dictate them from above,
and certainly not in advance. But at the time,
my business training told me this was the way
to proceed. The discussions went on at an
abstract level for months, the details over-
whelmed us, and we got nowhere.

In short, the early 1980s were a disaster.
After two years of stewing, it began to
dawn on me that my first reactions to most

situations were usually dead wrong. After all, my organizational instincts had brought us to Point A to begin with. Pursuing those instincts now would only bring us *back* to Point A. I needed to start thinking before I acted, and the thought I needed to think was, "Will this action help us achieve our new Point B?"

Point B also needed some revision. The early 1980s taught me that I couldn't give responsibility. People had to expect it, want it, even demand it. So my end state needed redefining. The goal was not so much a state of shared responsibility as an environment where people insist on being responsible.

To bring people to that new Point B, I had to learn to be a better coach. It took me additional years to learn the art of coaching, by which, in a nutshell, I mean communicating a vision and then getting people to see their own behavior, harness their own frustrations, and own their own problems.

Early in the change process, for example, I was told that workers in one plant disliked working weekends, which they often had to do to meet deliveries. Suspecting that the weekends weren't really necessary, I pressed plant managers to use the problem as an opportunity. I asked them if they had measured production efficiency, for instance, and if they had tried to get their workers to take responsibility for the overtime problem. The first thing everyone discovered was that machine down-time hovered between 30% and 40%. Then they started coming to terms with the fact that all that downtime had its causes—lateness, absences, sloppy maintenance, slow shift startups. Once the workers began to see that they themselves were the problem, they realized that they could do away with weekend work. In three weeks, they cut downtime to less than 10% and had Saturdays and Sundays off.

## MANAGING THE CONTEXT

The debacle of ordering change and watching it fail to occur showed me my limitations. I had come to realize that I didn't directly control the performance of the people at Johnsonville, that as a manager I didn't really manage people. They managed themselves.

But I did manage the context. I provided and allocated the resources. I designed and implemented the systems. I drew up and executed the organizational structure. The power of any contextual factor lies in its ability to shape the way people think and what they expect. So I worked on two contextual areas: systems and structures.

## Systems

I first attacked our quality control system. Quality was central to our business success, one of our key competitive advantages. But even though our quality was better than average, it wasn't yet good enough to be great.

We had the traditional quality control department with the traditional quality control responsibilities—catching errors before they got to the customer. Senior management was a part of the system. Several times a week we evaluated the product—that is to say, we *checked* it—for taste, flavor, color, and texture.

One day it struck me that by checking the product, top management had assumed responsibility for its quality. We were not encouraging people to be responsible for their own performance. We were not helping people commit themselves to making Johnsonville a great company.

This line of reasoning led me to another insight: the first strategic decision I needed to make was who should make decisions. On the theory that those who implement a decision and live with its consequences are the best people to make it, we changed our quality control system. Top management stopped tasting sausage, and the people who made sausage started. We informed line workers that from now on it would be their responsibility to make certain that only top-quality product left the plant. In the future, they would manage quality control.

It surprised me how readily people accepted this ownership. They formed teams of workers to resolve quality problems. For example, one team attacked the problem of leakers—vacuum-packed plastic packages of sausage that leaked air and shortened shelf life. The team gathered data, identified problems, worked with suppliers and with other line workers to develop and implement solutions, even visited retail stores to find out how retailers handled the product so we could make changes that would prevent their problems from occurring. The team took complete responsibility for measuring quality and then used those measurements to improve production processes. They owned and expected to own all the problems of producing top-quality sausage, and they wanted to do the best possible job. The results were amazing. Rejects fell from 5% to less than 0.5%.

Clearly this new quality control system was helping to create the end state we were after. Its success triggered changes in several other systems as well.

Teams of workers in other areas began to taste the product every morning and discuss possible improvements. They asked for information about costs and customer reactions, and we redesigned the information system to give it to them.

We began to forward customer letters directly to line workers. They responded to customer complaints and sent coupons for free Johnsonville sausage when they felt it was warranted. They came to own and expect responsibility for correcting the problems that customers raised in their letters.

People in each section on the shop floor began to collect data about labor costs, efficiency, and yield. They posted the data and discussed it at the daily tasting meeting.

Increasingly, people asked for more responsibility, and the information system encouraged them to take it. We were progressing
toward our end state, and as we made
progress we uncovered deeper and more
complex problems.

One of these arose when people on the
shop floor began to complain about fellow
workers whose performance was still slipshod or indifferent. In fact, they came to senior management and said, "You don't take
your own advice. If you did, you wouldn't let
these poor performers work here. It's your
job to either fix them or fire them."

Our first reaction was to jump in and do
something, but by now we had learned to
think before acting. We asked ourselves if

accepting responsibility for this problem would help us reach Point B. The answer was clearly no. More important, we asked ourselves who was in the best position to own the problem and came to the obvious conclusion that the people on the shop floor knew more about shop-floor performance than we did, so they were the best ones to make these decisions.

We offered to help them set performance standards and to coach them in confronting poor performers, but we insisted that since they were the production-performance experts, it was up to them to deal with the situation. I bit my tongue time and time again, but they took on the responsibility for dealing with performance problems and actually

fired individuals who wouldn't perform up to
the standards of their teams.

This led to a dramatic change in Johnsonville's human resource system. Convinced that inadequate selection and training
of new workers caused performance problems, line workers asked to do the selection
and training themselves. Managers helped
them set up selection and training procedures, but production workers made them
work. Eventually, line workers assumed most
of the traditional personnel functions.

The compensation system was another
early target for change. We had traditionally
given across-the-board annual raises like
most other businesses. What mattered was
longevity, not performance. That system was

also a stumbling block on our way to Point B, so we made two changes.

First, we eliminated the annual across-the-board raise and substituted a pay-for-responsibility system. As people took on new duties—budgeting, for instance, or training—they earned additional base income. Where the old system rewarded people for hanging around, regardless of what they contributed, the new one encouraged people to seek responsibility.

Second, we instituted what we called a "company performance share," a fixed percentage of pretax profits to be divided every six months among our employees. We based individual shares on a performance-appraisal system designed and administered by a volunteer team of line production workers from various departments. The system is explained in the insert "How Johnsonville Shares Profits on the Basis of Performance."

These system changes taught me two more valuable lessons. First, just start. Don't wait until you have all the answers. When I set out to make these changes, I had no clear picture of how these new systems would interact with one another or with other company systems and procedures, but if I had waited until I had all the answers, I'd still be waiting. A grand plan was impossible; there were too many variables. I wasn't certain which systems to change; I just knew I had to change something in order to alter expectations and begin moving toward my goal.

Second, start by changing the most visible system you directly control. You want your first effort to succeed. I knew I could control who tasted the product because I was doing the tasting. I also knew it was a highly visible action. Everyone waited to hear my taste-test results. By announcing that I wasn't going to taste the product anymore and that the people who made it were, everyone knew immediately that I was serious about spreading responsibility.

*Structures*

Along with the system changes, I introduced a number of changes in company structure. Teams gradually took over a number of the functions previously performed by individual managers in the chain of command, with the result that the number of hierarchical layers went from six to three.

Teams had already taken on responsibility for selecting, training, evaluating, and, when necessary, terminating fellow employees. Now they began to make all decisions about schedules, performance standards, assignments, budgets, quality measures, and capital improvements as well. In operations, teams assumed the supervisors' functions, and those jobs disappeared. Those former supervisors who needed authority in order to function left the company, but most went into other jobs at Johnsonville, some of them into technical positions.

The function of the quality control department was redefined. It stopped checking quality—now done by line workers—and began providing technical support to the production people in a cooperative effort to *improve* quality. The department developed systems for continuous on-line monitoring of fat, moisture, and protein content, for example, and it launched a program of outside taste testing among customers.

The traditional personnel department disappeared and was replaced by a learning and personal development team to help individual employees develop their own Points B and A—their destinations and starting points—and figure out how to use Johnsonville to reach their goals. We set up an educational allowance for each person, to be used however the individual saw fit. In the beginning, some took cooking or sewing classes; a few took flying lessons. Over time, however, more and more of the employees focused on job-related learning. Today more than 65% of all the people at Johnsonville are involved in some type of formal education.

The end state we all now envision for Johnsonville is a company that never stops learning. One part of learning is the acquisition of facts and knowledge—about accounting, machine maintenance, marketing, even about sky diving and Italian cooking. But the most important kind of learning teaches us to question our own actions and behavior in order to better understand the ways we perform, work, and live.

Helping human beings fulfill their potential is of course a moral responsibility, but it's also good business. Life is aspiration. Learning, striving people are happy people and good workers. They have initiative and imagination, and the companies they work for are rarely caught napping.

Learning is change, and I keep learning and relearning that change is and needs to be continuous. For example, our system and structural changes were reciprocal. The first led to the second, which then in turn led to new versions of the first.

Initially, I had hoped the journey would be as neat and orderly as it now appears on paper. Fortunately—since original mistakes are an important part of learning—it wasn't. There were lots of obstacles and challenges, much backsliding, and myriad false starts and wrong decisions.

For example, team leaders chosen by their team members were supposed to function as communication links, leaving the traditional management functions of planning and scheduling to the group itself. No sooner had the team leaders been appointed, however, than they began to function as supervisors. In other words, they immediately fell into the familiar roles they had always seen. We had neglected to give them and the plant managers adequate training in the new team model. The structure changed, but mind-sets didn't. It was harder to alter people's expectations than I had realized.

## INFLUENCING EXPECTATIONS

I discovered that change occurs in fits and starts, and that while I could plan individual changes and events, I couldn't plan the whole process. I also learned that expectations have a way of becoming reality, so I tried to use every available means— semantic, symbolic, and behavioral—to send messages that would shape expectations to Johnsonville's advantage.

For example, we wanted to break down the traditional pictures in people's minds of what managers do and how subordinates and

employees behave, so we changed the words
we used. We dropped the words employee
and subordinate. Instead we called everyone
a "member" of the organization, and managers became "coordinators" or "coaches."

Our promotion system had always sent a
powerful message: to move up the ladder you
need to become a manager and solve problems for your people. But this was now the
wrong message. I wanted coordinators who
could build problem-solving capacities in
others rather than solve their problems for
them. I recast the job requirements for the
people whose work I directly coordinated
(formerly known as "my management
team"), and they, in turn, did the same for
the people whose work they coordinated.

I took every opportunity to stress the need for coaching skills, and I continually de-emphasized technical experience. Whenever someone became a coordinator, I made sure word got around that the promotion was for demonstrated abilities as a teacher, coach, and facilitator.

This new promotion standard sent a new message: to get ahead at Johnsonville, you need a talent for cultivating and encouraging problem solvers and responsibility takers.

I discovered that people watched my every action to see if it supported or undermined our vision. They wanted to see if I practiced what I preached. From the outset I did simple things to demonstrate my sincerity. I made a sign for my desk that said

THE QUESTION IS THE ANSWER, and
when people came to me with questions,
I asked myself if they were questions I should
answer. Invariably, they weren't. Invariably,
people were asking me to make decisions for
them. Instead of giving answers, I turned the
tables and asked the questions myself, trying
to make them repossess their own problems.
Owning problems was an important part of
the end state I'd envisioned. I wasn't about
to let people give theirs to me.

I also discovered that in meetings people
waited to hear my opinion before offering
their own. In the beginning, I insisted they
say what they thought, unaware that I showed
my own preferences in subtle ways—my tone
of voice, the questions I asked—which,

nevertheless, anyone could read and interpret expertly. When I realized what was happening, I began to stay silent to avoid giving any clue to where I stood. The result was that people flatly refused to commit themselves to any decision at all. Some of those meetings would have gone on for days if I hadn't forced people to speak out before they'd read my mind.

In the end, I began scheduling myself out of many meetings, forcing others to make their decisions without me. I also stopped collecting data about production problems. I learned that if I had information about daily shortages and yields, I began to ask questions that put me firmly back in possession of the problems.

Eventually, I came to understand that everything I did and said had a symbolic as well as a literal meaning. I had to anticipate the potential impact of every word and act, ask myself again and again if what I was about to do or say would reinforce the vision or undermine it, bring us closer to Point B or circle us back to Point A, encourage people to own their own problems or palm them off on me. My job, as I had come to see it, was to put myself out of a job.

## WATERSHED

By mid-1985, we had all come a long way. Johnsonville members had started wanting and expecting responsibility for their own performance, and they usually did a good job. Return on assets was up significantly, as were margins and quality. But on the whole, the process of change had been a journey without any major mileposts or station stops. Then Palmer Sausage (not its real name) came along and gave us our watershed—a golden opportunity and a significant threat to our existence.

Palmer is a much larger sausage company that had contracted with us for private-label products during a strike in the early 1980s. Our quality was so high that they kept us on as a supplier after the strike ended. Now Palmer had decided to consolidate several facilities and offered to let us take over part of the production of a plant they were closing. It represented a huge increase in their order, and the additional business was very tempting: it could be very profitable, and it would justify the cost of a new and more efficient plant of our own. The upside was extremely attractive—if we could handle it.

That was what worried me. To handle an expanded Palmer contract, we'd have to hire and train a large group of people quickly and teach our present people new skills, keep quality high on both the Palmer products and our own, work six and seven days a week for more than a year until our new plant was ready, and run the risk if Palmer cancelled—which it could do on 30-days notice—of saddling ourselves with big layoffs and new

capacity we no longer had a market for.
Maybe it wasn't a bet-the-company decision,
but it was as close as I'd like to come.

Before 1982, I would have met for days
with my senior team to discuss all these
issues, and we would probably have turned
down the opportunity in the face of such an
overwhelming downside. But by 1985, it was
clear to me that the executive group was the
wrong group to make this decision. The
executives would not be responsible for
successfully implementing such a move.
The only way we could do Palmer successfully was if everyone at Johnsonville was
committed to making it work, so everyone
had to decide.

Until that moment, my senior team had
always made the strategic decisions. We took

advice from people in the operating departments, but the senior staff and I had dealt with the ultimate problems and responsibilities. We needed to move to a new level. This was a problem all of our people had to own.

My senior managers and I called a meeting of the entire plant, presented the problem, and posed three questions. What will it take to make it work? Is it possible to reduce the downside? Do we want to do it?

We asked the teams in each area to discuss these questions among themselves and develop a list of pros and cons. Since the group as a whole was too large to work together effectively, each team chose one member to report its findings to a plantwide representative body to develop a plantwide answer.

The small groups met almost immediately, and within days their representatives met. The discussion moved back and forth several times between the representative body and the smaller groups.

To make it work, the members decided we'd have to operate seven days a week, hire and train people to take new shifts, and increase efficiency to get more from current capacity. They also thought about the downside risk. The biggest danger was that we'd lose the added business after making all the investments and sacrifices needed to handle it. They figured the only way to reduce that downside potential was to achieve quality standards so high that we would actually improve the already first-rate Palmer product and, at the same time, maintain standards on our own products to make sure Johnsonville brands didn't fall by the wayside.

Two weeks later, the company decided almost unanimously to take the business. It was one of the proudest moments of my life. Left to our traditional executive decision making, we would have turned Palmer down. The Johnsonville people, believing in themselves, rose to the challenge. They really did want to be great.

The results surpassed our best projections. Learning took place faster than anticipated. Quality rose in our own product line as well as for Palmer. The new plant came on line in 1987. Palmer has come back to us several times since to increase the size of its orders even further.

## SUCCESS—THE GREATEST ENEMY

The pace of change increased after Palmer. Now that all of Johnsonville's people expected and wanted some degree of responsibility for strategic decisions, we had to redefine Point A, our current situation. The new level of involvement also led us to a more ambitious view of what we could ultimately achieve— Point B, our vision and destination.

We made additional changes in our career-tracking system. In our early enthusiasm, we had played down the technical aspects of our business, encouraging everyone to become a coordinator, even those who were far better suited to technical specialties. We also had some excellent salespeople who became coordinators because they saw it as the only path to advancement, though their talents and interests lay much more in selling than in coaching. When they became coordinators, we lost in three ways: we lost good salespeople, we created poor coordinators, and we lost sales from other good salespeople because they worked for these poor coordinators.

A career team recommended that Johnsonville set up dual career tracks—one for specialists and one for coordinators—that would enable both to earn recognition, status, and compensation on the basis of performance alone. The team, not the senior coordinators, agreed to own and fix the compensation problem.

Everyone at Johnsonville discovered they could do considerably better and earn considerably more than they had imagined. Since they had little trouble meeting the accelerated production goals that they themselves had set, members raised the minimum acceptable performance criteria and began routinely to expect more of themselves and others.

Right now, teams of Johnsonville members are meeting to discuss next year's capital budget, new product ideas, today's production schedule, and yesterday's quality, cost, and yield. More important, these same teams are redesigning their systems and structures to manage their continuing journey toward Point B, which, along with

Point A, they are also continually redefining. Most important of all, their general level of commitment is now as high or higher than my own.

In fact, our greatest enemy now is our success. Our sales, margins, quality, and productivity far exceed anything we could have imagined in 1980. We've been studied and written about, and we've spent a lot of time answering questions and giving advice. We've basked in the limelight, telling other people how we did it. All the time we kept telling ourselves, "We can't let this go to our heads." But of course it had already gone to our heads. We had begun to talk and brag about the past instead of about what we wanted for the future. Once we saw what we were doing, we managed to stop and, in the process, learn a lesson about the hazards of self-congratulation.

When I began this process of change ten years ago, I looked forward to the time when it would all be over and I could get back to my real job. But I've learned that change is the real job of every effective business leader because change is about the present and the future, not about the past. There is no end to change. This story is only an interim report.

Yet another thing I've learned is that the cause of excitement at Johnsonville Sausage is not change itself but the process used in producing change. Learning and responsibility are invigorating, and aspirations make our hearts beat. For the last five years, my own aspiration has been to eliminate *my* job by creating such a crowd of self-starting, problem-solving, responsibility-grabbing, independent thinkers that Johnsonville would run itself.

Two years ago, I hired a new chief operating officer and told him he should lead the company and think of me as his paid consultant. Earlier this year, he invited me to a management retreat, and I enjoyed myself. Other people owned the problems that had once been mine. My whole job was to generate productive conversations about Johnsonville's goals and to communicate its vision.

On the second evening of the retreat, I was given a message from my COO. There was a special session the next morning, he wrote, and added, "I want you there at 8:15."

Instinctively, it made me mad. Johnsonville was my company; I built it; I fixed it; he owed me his job. Who the hell did he think he was giving me orders like a hired consultant?

Then, of course, I laughed. It's not always easy giving up control, even when it's what you've worked toward for ten years. He wanted me there at 8:15? Well, good for him. I'd be there.

## How Johnsonville Shares Profits on the Basis of Performance

Every six months, we evaluate the performance of everyone at Johnsonville to help us compute shares in our profit-sharing program. Except "we" is the wrong word. In practice, performance evaluations are done by the employees themselves. For example, 300 wage earners—salaried employees have a separate profit-sharing pool and a different evaluation system—fill out forms in which they rate themselves on a scale of 1 to 9 in 17 specific areas grouped into three categories: performance, teamwork, and personal development.

Scores of 3, 4, or 5—the average range— are simply entered on the proper line. Low scores of 1 or 2 and high scores of 6 to 9 require a sentence or two of explanation.

Each member's coach fills out an identical form, and later both people sit down together and discuss all 17 areas. In cases of disagreement, the rule is only that their overall point totals must agree within nine points, whereupon

the two totals are averaged to reach a final
score. If they cannot narrow the gap to nine
points, an arbitration group is ready to step in
and help, but so far mediation has never been
needed.

All final scores, names deleted, are then
passed to a profit-sharing team that carves
out five categories of performance: a small
group of superior performers (about 5% of the
total), a larger group of better-than-average
workers (roughly 20%), an average group
amounting to about 50% of the total work
force, a below-average group of 20%, and a
small group of poor performers who are often
in some danger of losing their jobs.

The total pool of profits to be shared is then
divided by the number of workers to find an

average share—for the purpose of illustration, let's say $1,000. Members of the top group get a check for 125% of that amount or $1,250. Members of the next group get 110% ($1,100), of the large middle group, 100% or $1,000, and so on down to $900 and $750.

Yes, people do complain from time to time, especially if they think they've missed a higher share by only a point or two. The usual way of dealing with such situations is to help the individual improve his or her performance in enough areas to ensure a higher score the next time. But overall satisfaction with the system is very high, partly because fellow workers invented it, administer it, and constantly revise it in an effort to make it more equitable. The person currently in charge of the Johnsonville profit-sharing team is an hourly worker from the shipping department.

Many forms have been used over the years—a new one is under consideration at this moment—but the questions most recently asked, in a slightly edited version, are reprinted in this article.

---

## Johnsonville Foods, Inc.: Company Performance-Share Evaluation Form

Please check one: _____ Self _____ Coach

### I. PERFORMANCE

**A. Customer Satisfaction**
How do I rate the quality of the work I do?
Do I contribute my best to producing a product
to be proud of—one that I would purchase
or encourage someone else to purchase?                    Score _____

**B. Cost-Effectiveness**
To what extent do I perform my job in a
cost-effective manner? Do I strive to work
smarter? To work more productively with fewer

errors? To complete my job functions in a timely manner, eliminating overtime when possible? To reduce waste where possible in all departments?                               Score _____

## C. Attitude
To what extent do I have a positive attitude toward my personal, department, and company goals as expressed by my actions, feelings, and thoughts? Do I like to come to work? Am I thoughtful and considerate toward fellow members? Do I work to promote better attitudes? Do I demonstrate company loyalty?                               Score _____

## D. Responsibility
To what extent do I take responsibility for my own job? Do I accept a challenge? Do I willingly take on or look for additional responsibilities? Do I work independently of supervision?        Score _____

## E. Ideas
To what extent have I offered ideas and suggestions for improvements? Do I suggest better ways of doing things instead of just complaining?                               Score _____

## F. Problem Solver/Preventer
To what extent have I contributed to solving or preventing problems? Do I anticipate problem situations and try to avoid them? Do I push-pull when necessary? Do I keep an open line of communication?                               Score _____

## G. Safety
To what extent do my actions show my concern for safety for myself and others? Do I alert coworkers to unsafe procedures? Do I alert my coach to unsafe conditions in my department?     Score _____

**H. Quality Image**
To what extent have I displayed a high-quality
image in my appearance, language, personal
hygiene, and working environment?                    Score _____

## II. TEAMWORK

**A. Contribution to Groups**
How would I rate my contribution to my
department's performance? Am I aware
of department goals? Do I contribute to a
team? Do I communicate with team members?           Score _____

**B. Communication**
To what extent do I keep others informed to
prevent problems from occurring? Do I work
to promote communication between plants
and departments? Do I relay information to the
next shift? Do I speak up at meetings and let my
opinions and feelings be known?                      Score _____

**C. Willingness to Work Together**
To what extent am I willing to share the
responsibility of getting the work done?
Do I voluntarily assist others to obtain results?
Do I demonstrate a desire to accomplish
department goals? Do I complete paperwork
accurately and thoroughly and work toward
a smooth flow of information throughout
the company? Am I willing to share in any
overtime?                                            Score _____

**D. Attendance and Timeliness**
Do I contribute to the team by being present
and on time for work (including after breaks and
lunch)? Do I realize the inconvenience and
hardship caused by my absence or tardiness?          Score _____

## III. PERSONAL DEVELOPMENT

A. To what extent am I actively involved in lifelong learning? Taking classes is not the only way to learn. Other ways include use of our resource center or libraries for reading books, articles, etc.                                      Score _____

B. Do I improve my job performance by applying what I have learned?                                      Score _____

C. Do I ask questions pertaining to my job and other jobs too?                                      Score _____

D. Do I try to better myself not only through work but in all aspects of my life?                                      Score _____

E. Do I seek information about our industry?                                      Score _____

Total Points: _____

# Ralph Stayer's Guide to Improving Performance

Getting better performance from any group or individual, yourself included, means a permanent change in the way you think and run your business. Change of this kind is not a single transaction but a journey, and the journey has a specific starting point and a clear destination.

The journey is based on six observations about human behavior that I didn't fully grasp when I started, though I'd have made faster progress and fewer mistakes if I had.

1. People want to be great. If they aren't, it's because management won't let them be.

2. Performance begins with each individual's expectations. Influence what people expect and you influence how people perform.

3. Expectations are driven partly by goals, vision, symbols, semantics, and partly

by the context in which people work,
that is, by such things as compensation
systems, production practices, and
decision-making structures.

4. The actions of managers shape
   expectations.

5. Learning is a process, not a goal.
   Each new insight creates a new layer
   of potential insights.

6. The organization's results reflect me
   and my performance. If I want to
   change the results, I have to change
   myself first. This is particularly
   true for me, the owner and CEO,
   but it is equally true for every
   employee.

So to make the changes that will lead to great performance, I recommend focusing on goals, expectations, contexts, actions, and learning. Lee Thayer, a humanities professor at the University of Wisconsin, has another way of saying pretty much the same thing. He argues that since performance is the key to organizational success, management's job is to establish the conditions under which superb performance serves both the company's and individual's best interests.

CEOs need to focus first on changing themselves before they try to change the rest of the company. The process resembles an archaeological dig, or at least it did for me. As I uncovered and solved one problem, I almost invariably exposed another, deeper problem. As I gained one insight and mastered one situation, another situation arose that required new insight and more learning.

As I approached one goal, a new, more important, but more distant goal always began to take shape.

## NOTE

*I wish to acknowledge the contribution of my partner, James A. Belasco, to this article.*

## ABOUT THE AUTHOR

*Ralph Stayer* was, at the time this article
was first published, the CEO of Johnsonville
Foods in Sheboygan, Wisconsin, and the
managing partner of Leadership Dynamics,
a consulting group that specializes in
change.

# Article Summary

## The Idea in Brief

Do your employees work together like a strikingly synchronized flock of geese on the wing—sharing a goal, taking turns leading, and mastering the task at hand? Or do they seem more like a herd of buffalo—blindly following their leader and passively standing around waiting for instructions?

Ralph Stayer, head of family-owned Johnsonville Sausage, asked himself this question—and realized he led a bunch of buffalo who were wallowing toward extinction. His employees were bored, made dumb mistakes, and didn't care—a dangerous scenario, considering the formidable competitors sniffing around Johnsonville's turf.

Stayer took action. He fixed *himself* first—by refusing to own every problem and make every decision. And he stopped expecting his people to be incapable. Then he fixed *employees*—getting them to seize ownership of Johnsonville's problems and *insist* on taking responsibility for themselves and the business.

Stayer's reward? Employees became such self-starting, problem-solving, responsibility-grabbing, independent thinkers that Johnsonville nearly ran itself without him. But the true test came when a longstanding, key customer offered Johnsonville a major, risky—and potentially highly profitable—contract. Employees answered with a resounding "Yes!"—and performed like pros.

# The Idea in Practice

## *Don't Manage People—Manage Systems and Structures Instead*

People can manage themselves—if *you* manage their work *context*; i.e., the *systems* (quality control, performance assessment, compensation) and *structures* (teams, departments) that shape people's thinking and behavior and push the organization toward its ideal.

**Systems:** Start by changing the *most visible* systems you directly control.

*Example:* Stayer himself checked sausage quality by tasting it—a highly visible quality-control system. This kept workers from taking responsibility for their own performance. But when Stayer upended the quality-control system—inviting sausage-making line workers to taste it themselves—they embraced this ownership. They formed teams to resolve quality problems, and rejects fell from 5% to an amazing 0.5%.

*Example:* When shop-floor workers complained about slipshod fellow workers, Stayer invited them to solve the problem. They took on the selection and training of new workers—gradually assuming traditional personnel functions, including firing. Shop-floor performance soared.

**Structures:** Seize opportunities to make structural changes based on successful system changes.

*Example:* Stayer replaced Johnsonville's traditional personnel department with a learning and personal development team and employee-education allowance. More than 65% of employees now take part in formal education. Staffed by people with imagination, initiative, and competitive edge, Johnsonville "never stops learning."

### *Influence Employee Expectations*

Use every available means—semantic, symbolic, behavioral—to shape employees' expectations about what it takes to succeed.

*Example:* Stayer recast promotion standards, downplaying technical skill and emphasizing coaching and teaching instead. The move sent a new message: To succeed at Johnsonville, you must cultivate problem solvers and responsibility takers.

*Example:* When Stayer realized others were second-guessing him in meetings, he scheduled himself out of most gatherings. His absence forced others to make decisions themselves—and own their own problems. His *new* job? To put himself out of a job.